Poetry 3

Series Editor: Pie Corbett

CAMBRIDGE UNIVERSITY PRESS
Cambridge, New York, Melbourne, Madrid, Cape Town, Singapore, São Paulo

Cambridge University Press
The Edinburgh Building, Cambridge CB2 8RU, UK

www.cambridge.org
Information on this title: www.cambridge.org/9780521618847

First published 2005
Reprinted 2006, 2007

Printed in the United Kingdom at the University Press, Cambridge

A catalogue record for this publication is available from the British Library

ISBN 978-0-521-61884-7 paperback

ACKNOWLEDGEMENTS

Cover: Bill Ledger

Photos: p. 2 Ardea.com

Artwork: Bill Ledger, Beehive Illustration (Mark Ruffle, Russell Becker, Jim Peacock)

Texts: 'Just Wait', © 2000 Valerie Bloom, from *The World is Sweet,* published by Bloomsbury Children's Books, reprinted by permission of Valerie Bloom; 'Weather Zoo', 'Unicorn', 'Drum Beat' © Pie Corbett; 'Eat Me' © Jan Dean 2005; 'The Car Park Cat' and 'Six o'Clock Fox' from *Picture a Poem* by Gina Douthwaite, published by Red Fox and reprinted by permission of the The Random House Group Ltd; 'Riddle Me Scares' © John Foster 2004 from *Our Teacher's Gone Bananas* (Oxford University Press), included by permission of the author; 'The Wizard's Dragon' © John Foster 2005; 'The Schoolkids' Rap' © John Foster 2001 from *Word Wizard* (Oxford University Press) included by permission of the author; 'What's in the Cellar?', 'Down by the School Gate', 'Football' and 'Crocodiles' © Wes Magee; 'Words to Whisper' and 'The Alphabet Zoo' © Michaela Morgan; 'Dragons' Wood' from *Barking Back at Dogs: Poems by Brian Moses* (Macmillan 2000) © Brian Moses 2000; 'Zoo of Winds' from *Taking Out the Tigers: Poems by Brian Moses* (Macmillan 2005) © Brian Moses 2005; 'An Unlikely Alphabet of Animals in Even Unlikelier Places', 'Is the Sun a Star?' and 'Questions about Slowworms' © Brian Moses 2005; 'Me 'n' My Magic Football Boots' and 'Funky Football' from *Kick It! – Football Poems by Nick Toczek* (Macmillan Children's Books, 2002).

Contents

Shape
and
observation

Car bonnet cat
keeping warm, car bonnet cat
with crocodile yawn, stares from his sand-
peppered forest of fluff, segment-of-lemon eyes warning,
ENOUGH!   Just draw back that hand, retreat,   ***GO AWAY***!
and his claws flex a tune to say: I won't play but I'll spit
like the sea whipped wild in a gale, hump up like a wave,
flick a forked-lightning tail, lash out and scratch at
your lobster-pink face, for no-one, ***but no-one***,
removes from this place, car bonnet cat
keeping warm, car bonnet cat
by the name of
STORM.

Gina Douthwaite

Six o'Clock Fox

Cop-
per coat
ablaze, tail brushing stubble, he stalks,
pauses … picking paws he pricks signal ears,
directs wet pebble eyes beyond his
twitch of whiskers. Freeze-framed, he
holds   the moment,   then sweeps
to   streak   towards
the   swell
-ing   sun.

Gina Douthwaite

What's in the Cellar?

Holed buckets, bald brooms.
Cobwebbed wine bottles.
A rusty rat trap.
Painted gazunders.
A fireguard. A kettle.
Pile of damp coal.
Ripped, mouldy books.

Top hat in a box.
Plonk, claret and hocks.
Old mantelpiece clocks.
Stuffed head of a fox.
Pine chest crammed with frocks.
A score of odd socks.
Chinese chopsticks and woks.

And
something's
moaning,
something's
groaning...

False teeth in a jar.
Soiled, motheaten quilt.
Limescaled brass pans.
A Victorian mangle.
The skull of a cat.
A cradle. A cot.
Torn Man. U. shirt.

A splintered teak door.
One snaggle-toothed saw.
The tusk of a boar.
Shells from the seashore.
Blunt knives in a drawer.
One furred apple core.
Blood stains on the floor.

And
something's
glaring,
something's
staring...

Wes Magee

Zoo of Winds

Wild winds have escaped tonight,
and like animals suddenly loose from a zoo
they are out doing damage.
We hear them snaking
into cracks and crevices
while beasts
with the strength of buffaloes
batter the building.

Shrill birds whistle through the hallway
and a lion's roar seems stuck
in the chimney.
A howling hyena is caught
in the porch
while a horrid hook of a claw
tries to splinter the loft hatch.

All manner of fearsome creatures
lunge down the lane
while our garden is buffeted
by the angry breath of bears.
I hope someone soon
recaptures these beasts,
locks them away,
cages them tightly.
These winds are not welcome visitors,
not tonight, not any time.

Brian Moses

Weather Zoo

When the thunder thuds,
 The elephant
     Blows its grey trumpet
  And stamps its creased feet
Like tree trunks thumping.

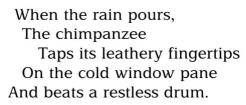

When the hailstones patter,
 The mongoose
     Tapdances on tiptoes
         And the squirrel monkey slips by,
  Spitting out melon pips
Like tiny black bullets,
As fast as full stops.

When the rain pours,
 The chimpanzee
     Taps its leathery fingertips
  On the cold window pane
And beats a restless drum.

When the snow falls,
 The white moth
     Flutters its dusty wings,
  Frail as rice paper,
Like soft Chinese silk.

Pie Corbett

Dragons' Wood

We didn't see dragons
in Dragons' Wood
but we saw
where the dragons had been.

We saw tracks in soft mud
that could only have been scratched
by some sharp-clawed creature.

We saw scorched earth
where fiery dragon breath
had whitened everything to ash.

We saw trees burnt to charcoal.
We saw dragon dung
rolled into boulders.

And draped from a branch
we saw sloughed off skin,
scaly, still warm…

We didn't see dragons
in Dragons' Wood,
but this was the closest
we'd ever been

to believing.

Brian Moses

The Wizard's Dragon

I am the wizard's dragon.
I speak with tongues of flame.
I am the wizard's dragon.
Firesnorter is my name.

I guard the room where he keeps
His secret book of spells.
I guard the dungeons where he keeps
His demons in their cells.

Day and night I keep watch
As I patrol the skies,
Searching out intruders
With my penetrating eyes.

Scattered round the castle's grounds
Are the bones of those who've died,
Scorched to death by my fiery breath
As they tried to get inside.

I am the wizard's dragon.
I speak with tongues of flame.
I am the wizard's dragon.
Firesnorter is my name.

John Foster

Unicorn

I am the Wizard's Unicorn.

I speak in soft clouds
as white as flowing milk.

I guard the palace
where doves flutter in each room
like trapped moths in a jar.

I watch the distant rivers
and see the polar bears
scoop salmon from the icy water.

I listen to the doors' creak
and the echo of footsteps
as ghostly chains rattle.

I eat paper torn from a book of spells
and chalk dug from the hillside.

I touch the snow as it melts,
as cold as frosted stars.

I smell the scent of a princess's skin.

I hope for freedom
and to run the open hills.

Because, I am the Wizard's Unicorn.

Pie Corbett

Performance

Words to Whisper

Words to whisper…
Words to **SHOUT**.
To pack a punch!
To cast a doubt…
Words to relish
Words to chew.
Antique words
or words brand new.
Words to clacker and to clack
like trains that travel on a track.
Words to soothe, words to sigh
to shush and hush and *lullaby*.
Words to tickle or to tease
to murmur, hum or buzz like bees.
Words like hubbub, splash and splutter
wiffle, waffle, murmur, mutter.
Words that babble like a stream
Words to **SNAP!** when you feel mean.
Get lost! Drop dead! Take a hike!
Shut it! Beat it! On your bike!
Cruel words that taint and taunt.
Eerie words that howl and haunt.
Words with rhythm. Words with rhyme.
Words to make you feel just fine.
To clap your hands, tap your feet
or click your fingers to the beat.
Words to make you grow – or cower.
Have you heard the word?
        WORDPOWER

Michaela Morgan

Down by the School Gate

There goes the bell.
It's half past three –
And down by the school gate
You will see…

Ten mums talk talk talking,
Nine babies squawk squawking,
   Eight toddlers all squabbling,
  Seven Grans on bikes wobbling,
Six cars stopping, parking,
Five dogs bark bark, barking,
   Four child-minders running,
   Three bus drivers sunning,
Two teenagers dating,
One lollipop man waiting…

The school is out.
It's half past three,
And the first to the school gate
… is ME!

Wes Magee

The Schoolkids' Rap

Miss was at the blackboard writing with the chalk,
When suddenly she stopped in the middle of her talk.
She snapped her fingers – snap! snap! snap!
Pay attention children and I'll teach you how to rap.

She picked up a pencil, she started to tap.
All together children, now clap! clap! clap!
Just get the rhythm, just get the beat.
Drum it with your fingers, stamp it with your feet.

That's right children, keep in time.
Now we've got the rhythm, all we need is the rhyme.
This school is cool. Miss Grace is ace.
Strut your stuff with a smile on your face.

Snap those fingers, tap those toes.
Do it like they do it on the video shows.
Flap it! Slap it! Clap! Snap! Clap!
Let's all do the schoolkids' rap!

John Foster

Me 'n' My Magic Football Boots

We're in league, in cahoots

Me 'n' my magic
Me 'n' my magic
Me 'n' my magic football boots.

There's no other footwear suits.
In rhyming slang, my daisy roots,
Got no match, no substitutes.

Me 'n' my magic
Me 'n' my magic
Me 'n' my magic football boots.

Football chants and whoops and hoots
And wild applause and drums and flutes
And rattle clatters, whistle toots.

Me 'n' my magic
Me 'n' my magic
Me 'n' my magic football boots.

Watch which move each executes
Spot their separate attributes,
Left one tackles, right one shoots.

Me 'n' my magic
Me 'n' my magic
Me 'n' my magic football boots.

Nick Toczek

Funky Football

Sock it to me
Sock it to me
Sock-sock-soccer it

Root-ti-toot
Y'go shoot, shoot, shoot
Shoot, shoot, shoot
With your football boot

We're losing now
But let's get cute
And turn the tide
Like King Canute
Let's win this game
And reap the fruit
Clean as a whistle
Clear as a flute

Root-ti-toot
Y'go shoot, shoot, shoot
Shoot, shoot, shoot
With your football boot

So sock it to me
Sock it to me
Sock-sock-soccer it

Root-ti-toot
Y'go shoot, shoot, shoot
Shoot, shoot, shoot
With your football boot

It's in the bag
The game's a beaut
It's a long loud laugh
It's hoot, hoot, hoot
So keep your cool
Be resolute
Goals are what
We'll execute

Root-ti-toot
Y'go shoot, shoot, shoot
Shoot, shoot, shoot
With your football boot

So sock it to me
Sock it to me
Sock-sock-soccer it

Root-ti-toot
Y'go shoot, shoot, shoot
Shoot, shoot, shoot
With your football boot

Nick Toczek

Just Wait

Ah goin' to live in a de forest,
Just meself an' me,
Ah goin' to run away when it get light,
Just you wait an' see.

Nobody goin' be there to tell me
Not to paint me toenail red,
Which dress, or blouse, or skirt to wear,
Or what time to go to bed.

Nobody goin' be there to criticise,
Ah goin' be on me own,
Nobody to frown an' make a fuss,
To groan an' gripe an' moan.

Me chair goin' to be a tree stump,
Me bed, banana trash,
Ah goin' eat me food out o' cocoa leaf,
Drink from a calabash.

Ah goin' brush me teeth with chew stick,
An' wash me face with dew,
Ah goin' use withes to make ribbon,
An' coconut husk make shoes.

Ah goin' swim like turtle in the river,
Swing from the highes' tree,
In fact, ah think ah goin' go right now.

But first, let me see what on TV.

Valerie Bloom

Drum Beat

The thunder came –
Roaring and thumping,
Rushing and jumping.

The storm, the storm.
Stay in; keep warm!

The wind came –
Hushing and hurrying,
Splashing and scurrying.

The storm, the storm.
Stay in; keep warm!

The rain came –
Spitting and moaning,
Snarling and groaning…

And in came –

My cat … purring –

The storm, the storm.
Stay in; keep warm!

Pie Corbett

Language Play

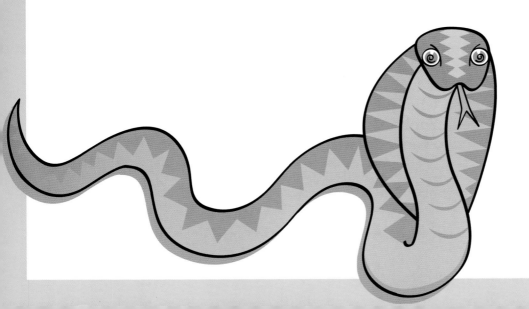

The Alphabet Zoo

There are angry ants and antelopes
And birds, baboons and bees.
There are cockatoos and camels,
And dingo dogs with fleas.
There are finny fish and funny frogs,
A gorilla who is blue.
There are giggling goats and natty gnats
– and is that a gnu?
There are hungry hippos, horses and a happy hen.
There are insects and iguanas. (Count them. There are ten.)
There are jaguars who jump,
Kangaroos who kick,
And little lambs with lollies that they like to lick.
There are mammoths, moths and monsters,
Nightingales and a newt.
There's an ostrich and an octopus (she likes the water chute).
There are penguins and pet parrots
And quite a quiet queen bee.
There's a rat who races round and roars as ratty as can be.
There are six sad snakes who slide and slip,
Ten timid toads (dark brown).
There's an uppity umbrella bird, who is hanging upside down.
There's a vole, a vulture and a vampire bat
And a wiggly worm or two.
There's an x-ray fish who goes splish splish
And a yak who yells **Yoohoo!**
There are zebras who zoom about, in a zippy, zigzag way.

They are the alphabet zoo
And they'd like to see you
So
COME TO THE ALPHABET ZOO TODAY!

Michaela Morgan

An Unlikely Alphabet of Animals in Even Unlikelier Places

Aylesbury is the area for aardvarks
and Bellingham is brimming with bees.
In Carlisle you'll come across caterpillars
and in Doncaster, donkeys.
In Egham, elephants are everywhere
while in Frome all you'll find are frogs.
Grimsby is great for goats
and Hastings is home to hot dogs!
In the Isle of Islay I spied iguanas
and in Jarrow I juggled with jellyfish.
In Kirklees I was kind to koalas
but llamas in London were loutish.
Meercats have moved into Margate
and Newbury is well known for newts.
Orang-utans are oafish in Oxford
and penguins in Penge wear playsuits.
Quetzals are quiet in Queenborough
but rhinos are roaring in Rochdale.
Squirrels surf in the sea off St Ives
while turtles in Taunton tell tales.
Umbrella birds unwind in Ullapool
while vipers are venomous in Villaze.
Wildebeests wait in Warrington
for X-ray fish Xeroxing x-rays.
Yaks yawn in Yarmouth and long for their beds
and all you'll get from zebras in Zennor are zzzzzs.

Brian Moses

Crocodiles

Crocodiles
are **R**eally cunning fighters.
With m**O**nstrous,
Crushing jaws
and awes**O**me teeth
they're **D**readful biters.
In murky swamps
they f**L**oat
then sudd**E**nly attack,
the blighter**S**.

Wes Magee

Football

F ootballers who foul will be sent of **F**.
O ften they leave to a loud bo **O**.
O r, at least, ironic cheers as they g **O**.
T op players need a steady temperamen **T**.
B ody fitness is an essential: no fla **B**.
A rsenal are sometimes as boring as Siberi **A**.
L eft wingers dribble with the bal **L**.
L ast minute shot can mean … a goa **L**!

Wes Magee

Eat Me

I'm harder than mud
But softer than rocks
Yellow as buttercups
Smelly as socks.
Eat me with crackers
As much as you please.
Though I have no muscles
I'm very strong _____ .

Jan Dean

Riddle Me Scares

My first is in ghoul and also in charm.
My second is in magic and twice in alarm.
My third is in cauldron but isn't in fire.
My fourth is in gremlin but not in vampire.
My fifth is in skeleton and in bones.
My sixth is in werewolf but isn't in groans.
My seventh is in spell but not in broomstick.
My eighth's found in treat, but not found in trick.
My ninth is in phantom but isn't in fear.
My whole is the scariest night of the year.

John Foster

Is the Sun a Star?

(55% of people interviewed didn't know that the sun is a star.)

There's a rumour going round
that the sun is a star,

But I haven't seen the sun
in gossip magazines.

I haven't seen the sun on chat shows
or making videos.

I haven't seen the sun wearing shades
or holding a microphone.

Maybe its message
isn't getting across,
maybe it uses
the wrong PR.

If the sun is a star
then why don't we see it
waving from the back
of a stretch limousine?

Is it the star of the stage
or star of the screen?

Does it moonwalk daily
across the sky?

Does it drop-kick a ball
through the Gates of Heaven?

There's a rumour going round
that the sun's a star

but that's one rumour
too far…

Brian Moses

Questions about Slowworms

Is a slowworm slow
or can he be fast?
On sports days would he
always come last?
Is a slowworm too slow
to meet a mate?
Does he always turn up
late for a date?

I wonder how you tell
a boy from a girl?
When he falls in love
is his head in a whirl?
Does he hear love songs
and feel heartache?
Does he ever wish
he were really a snake?

Does he envy the glow
that a glowworm makes?
Does he have regrets?
Does he make mistakes?
Or is he content
with a warm sunny place?
Is that a smile we can see
on his face?

Brian Moses